CITY CANYONS

Poems
by

Alice Elizabeth Rogoff

BLUE LIGHT PRESS ◆ 1ST WORLD PUBLISHING

SAN FRANCISCO ◆ FAIRFIELD ◆ DELHI

City Canyons

Copyright ©2024 by Alice Elizabeth Rogoff

All rights reserved. Printed in the United States of America. No part of this book may be used or reproduced in any manner whatsoever without written permission except in the case of brief quotations embodied in critical articles and reviews. For information contact:

1st World Library
PO Box 2211
Fairfield, IA 52556
www.1stworldpublishing.com

Blue Light Press
www.bluelightpress.com
bluelightpress@aol.com

Book & Cover Design
Melanie Gendron
melaniegendron999@gmail.com

Cover Art
Melanie Gendron

Author Photo
David H. Williams

First Edition

Library of Congress Cataloging-in-Publication Data

ISBN: 978-1-4218-3555-6

CITY CANYONS

Table of Contents

Turned Back 1
Paul Robeson's Voice 2
Keys 3
Syria Page Two 4
International 5
Dancing in the Street 6
Synchronicity 7
Common Denominator 8
Have the Children Found Their Parents Yet? 9
Corona Subconscious 10
Ralph 12
Subscribers 13
To Ronnie Goodman 14
Ghost Ships and Ateliers 15
The Long Gray Blanket 16
Cold 17
Dolores Park 18
Cornbread 19
The Detroit Stairway 20
Perhaps to Dream 21
In Between 22
After the Park Branch Library Poetry Reading 23
Outside My Cottage 24
Albion 25
The Building on Bartlett Street 26
Barcelona 27

Hydra	28
Uxmal	29
Bluebird	30
Tamaracks	31
Call It Bloom	32
Snow-scape	33
Without Warmth	34
Thunderstorms in San Francisco	35
My Father's Funeral	37
Photos	38
The Presses	39
Cherry Soup	40
David	41
Strabismus	43
Lurilla and Lavender Girl	45
Corky	46
You	47
Escaping Fire	48
Under	49
Skeleton	50
Woman Having a Mask Made of Her Face	51
Playing Solitaire	53
My Woman's Id	54
Untitled	55
Sunrise Ritual	56
To Be a Witch	57
The Woman Climber on Annapurna	58
Wild Nights	59

Crossing the River	60
Stations	61
Wall of Roses	62
The Peace Rose	63
War or Peace?	64
The Five of Us	65
Firmament	66
In the Forest	67
Glen Park	68
Ten Lakes	69
Earth Day	71
The White Ducks	72
The Vole	74
Going to Jupiter	76
We Seahorses	77
Diatoms	78
After Coming Back from Big Sur	79
The Tall Trees	80
Strategy	81
Romance of the Porch	82
The Feral Puppy	83
Why I Can't Spell Graffiti and Other Musings	84
Communication	85
Learning the Alphabet	86
Lesson in Jazz	87
Bajone's	88
Miles	89
Love Sessions	90

In Transit	91
The Trieste Café	92
In the Workers' Café	93
Marble, Colorado	94
The Lights on Broadway	95
Buried Treasure	96
Louis'	98
Mesmerized	100
Ocean	101
Acknowledgements	103
About the Author	105

Turned Back

How did I feel when the boat turned around?
When the waves came over the bow,
When I felt like I was drowning.
When I did drown?
When they signed the order?
When the government sent me back?
When the boat left the American shore
And I went back in a camp?
Because the boat turned around.
When life stopped –
How did I feel when the boat turned around?
When Marta joined me
On a border
In limbo,
On a passage from limbo to hell,
How does Marta feel
Turning around,
Turning back,
With two little children,
Juan and Felipe?
Turning back,
Back,
Back.

Paul Robeson's Voice

I am hearing
The disappeared voice
Of Paul Robeson
Singing "Water Boy,"
Calls on a chain gang
In the hot south.
I am hearing
The disappearing
In America's prisons,
The disappearing
Islands covered
With lapping rising waters,
Heavy hurricanes
In New Orleans,
Paul Robeson
Changing the words
Of "Old Man River,"
Paul Robeson
For Global Unity,
Global warming
Getting hotter,
A laborer in the hot sun
In Flint, Michigan,
A farm worker
In Watsonville
Needing water
In a pandemic,
Paul Robeson
Calls to a young prisoner,
Too young,
On a hot day,
Too hot,
Red flag warnings.

Keys

She had a key
To the door once.
Did she drop it when she left?
Her grandmother had a key too.
Grandma buried it deep in the soil.
The door is missing now.
At least that one is in Krakow.
A brother has the key
To the door in Ramallah.

"How long do keys last?"
Asked a little girl.
"As long as one can remember
The way to go back home,"
Her Grandma said.
"And what if you can't go back to a home?"
The little girl asked.
They are the keys to one's heart.

Syria Page Two

I've found the war this morning
as it is each morning.
I will never go there
to that war-torn country
I see on page two,
to see the rubble
scattered remains
of houses
grey on black and white.
Somewhere out of the photo
there may be people
beyond the dwellings
once lit,
once cooking
lamb or figs
with children,
grandmothers.
Their pictures
are streams of refugees
not on page 2,
now not on the grey
newsprint at all.
So, another day,
Wednesday, Thursday,
another morning,
I look for Syria,
Page Two.

International

Along a Greek roadside
A woman with a muslin bag
Picks wild thyme
Wild scallions,
Nasturtium blossoms,
Any edible grasses.
Athenians stand on street corners
Waiting for a job
Amid unfinished buildings
Near ancient Greek monuments.
So many without food in U.S. cities
And I remember
Along the roads
People picking
Wild onion,
Wild cabbage
As I give away a dollar
On 101 South.

Dancing in the Street

Referring to a recent news story of an African-American man arrested while dancing in the street on the theme of thumb from a prompt.

Thumbelina
Dances in the street
(If one will let her.)
She's not very big,
But she dances
In the early morning.
Some see her,
To their delight
Pirouetting,
But one day,
She is snatched up
And arrested for
Disturbing the peace,
Being unusual,
Too small, too
Turning,
Her small feet leaping.
Her neighbors though
Make a circle
Around Thumbelina
To protect her from the police.
Thumbelina dance, dance, dance.

Synchronicity

Over the fence,
The fig tree leaf
And rose bush flowers
Move closer and closer
To each other.
The green and red
Are lit up by the sun.
In synchronicity,
The two flora
Join together, June first,
The day after
The marches and protests
For George Floyd's
Murder by police.
It all comes together
And what does
It all say,
Each day the
Rose and fig leaf
Reach out more?
One thing beautiful
In how disturbing
Life has become.

Common Denominator

In Togo,
Before school
The children
Drum each day,
Finding their rhythm,
And one
Child's favorite
Game is
Wari,
Based on math;
And when one
Does not have
A carved
Wari board
One can play
With bowls
Dug in the ground.
Now, during Covid,
Statistics
Jump out at me,
Big numbers,
Somewhat
Forgetting
In Africa,
Children die
Of malaria
Every day
Without the
Numbers
Being counted
For all.

Have the Children Found Their Parents Yet?

Years ago,
She was confined in a cage.
Still in another cage
Of separation,
Put on a treadmill
Jumble of paperwork
While parents gone
Declared illegal
Children floating
In ocean of tears
Bonding in limbo
Harsh crossing –
What does family friendly mean?
Has she found her parents yet?
Or is she number 510
Unreunited?

Corona Subconscious

When I was a teenager
Going barefoot
Into our cold basement
I remember my father was so mad
At me
For going barefoot,
It didn't seem so serious,
I could get sick he said.
Now, this early May
As I walk through the woods
With a mask
Thinking about his birthday
May sixteenth 1910,
In 1913,
His little brother
Died of spinal meningitis
Before penicillin,
Some walkers without masks
And not at a distance,
I thought Dad's anger
Was a businessman
Encountering a fresh flower child,
But now I think
It touched off
Something in him
Like the dark inside
Of an old tree,
What was it that went wrong?
– They both were so little –
That a little child
Could disappear
Without a trace?

Before he even really knew
His little brother?
Before they could play together
In the sun and snow.

Ralph

In the cemetery in Queens,
I could not find my
Father's little brother Ralph.
On the convoluted New York roads,
I got lost going to it,
Just as Ralph had gotten lost
In family history,
A baby who died of
Spinal meningitis
In an epidemic.
The local people helping
To find the cemetery.
The cemetery map says
Ralph is there,
Yet the names from 1913
Are too difficult to read.
I am helped
To rub the stones.
Ralph may be one of 2
Of the 25 small graves.
After Ralph died,
A marriage fell apart.
Later there was a marriage
For 50 years
And more children
Who never knew Ralph.
My parents only spoke of him once,
Leaving Ralph, who would have been all alone
If not for the other
Babies and toddlers,
Like so many, with a
Sculpture of a little lamb
On top of a tiny stone,
Almost erased.

Subscribers

Hastening towards the symphony
Walking along the sidewalk,
A little flame lights up,
Four men on my right side in the dark
Getting ready to shoot up,
Or smoke,
Take fentanyl.
I'm on my way to hear
Beethoven or Bach,
I shoot a glance
Towards the men's direction
And keep walking fast,
Look down at my feet for needles,
I hurry to hear music, the Magnificat,
Schumann, Schubert,
What is it this time?
Funny, I didn't know until later
That two operations I had
Used fentanyl, too,
For one of them, the doctor said
It would burn,
It hurt as I closed my eyes
And went to sleep.
The symphony crowd
Rushes forward and we bathe in sound.

To Ronnie Goodman – a homeless artist

Ronnie
Is running
To run to get
His art
From being
Run over,
Carted away
In trucks rumbling.
Ronnie was running
To sketch, to
Print, to paint,
Black lines, or lives.
Lives.
Running over
Sidewalk cracks,
Feet moving, stepping,
Sitting for a moment.
Ronnie is bicycling,
The pedals drawing
Circles on Sixteenth Street.

The Fourth Amendment to the United States Constitution states people have a right "to be secure in their persons, houses, papers and effects against unreasonable searches and seizures."

Ghost Ships and Ateliers

Perhaps she was Mimi,
and he was Rodolfo
lying on pallets,
and Marcello
painting in a cold garret
or fiery third floor
no escaping
when the Reaper comes,
Rodolfo's poetry blending into smoke
and Mimi's curtailed breath,
scattered paints and brushes
above a Parisian-Oakland atelier
in a studio
where Rodolfo and Mimi fall in love,
and Mimi dies.
Final words, au revoir,
holding a palette full of colors.
They were Mimi,
and Rodolfo
and their friend Marcello.
It was home
in spite of it
all,
or because of it.

The Long Gray Blanket

On the subway,
There he is again
The man with the long gray blanket,
Walking down the aisle,
Pushing through the car door,
Covered by the blanket
Down to his heels,
Frayed at the bottom and the top.
Perhaps he could be the same man
I saw two months ago
Or is he only dressed in the identical blanket,
Like the one I have lying in a trunk,
Used for cold summer evenings
On camping trips when I was young,
Pine needles and dried Scotch broom
Still scattered on the heavy gray cloth
That lay on the ground,
Smoky, still lingering from campfires,
Another thing forgotten in my mother's attic.
The man in the subway car
Paces back and forth,
His arm holding the wrapped blanket close,
Not revealing much.
He doesn't say anything
As he walks back and forth,
Wearing a lost childhood.

Cold

On a cold day
In San Francisco,
In Union Square,
Grannies sing
Against war;
A woman at a Mission bus stop
Asks where she can
Buy a blanket,
I don't usually shop at big stores,
She wants one nice
But not costly,
I point to Cliff's five and dime –
We do what we can
To keep warm.

Dolores Park

Where have the congas in
Dolores Park gone?
I was living above the park
Drummers' hands sending beats
Through an open window
From a park named for sorrow
The old Jewish cemetery
Where the earthquake fires stopped
The drums an unlawful language once
Dawn foggy voices
Of Africans, Spanish Sephardim
Sounds of the Mission
The Mission slipping away
Like the underground creek
Buried.
One day the conga players
Stopped playing
In Dolores Park
But I hear them in
My memory,
The rhythms carried
Through an open window.

Cornbread

Uptown,
Ten blocks
On the north side of Chicago,
Migrants from Kentucky,
Appalachia,
After-school program
At Hull House,
Gathering around a stove
For cooking class
Where I put together
A cornbread,
Melting butter,
Pouring corn meal,
"We have that at home,"
One child says,
No need to teach them really,
It comes out of the oven,
The recipe says golden brown,
None of them leaves,
Ten little children
Gathered around the stove
And cornbread.

Hull House is now shut down
The large apartments
Changed to Cambodian,
Latinx and Black.
And now, the Uptown neighborhood
Has a different name
The apartments modernized,
With new sinks and stoves.

The Detroit Stairway

The Detroit stairway
Goes up to where I don't know.
Like life, it is supposed
To go to some destination
But I cannot see the top,
One can hardly see
The whole staircase itself.
Is there a mountain lion
On the top
Who is rambling
Through a city?
Or a raccoon
Scavenging for food?
A friendly dog?
The house that wasn't in code
And fell down?
When you reach the top
And turn around
What will you see?
The moon, the mountains,
Or the little boxes houses
All in a row?
Will you be going up or
Down
Or standing still
In the middle of it all?

Perhaps to Dream

From the people about me,
The smell of cooking,
The life of an apartment house,
With the stairs and hallways
I stay alive here
Sniffing the aromas
That drift about me.

Sleeping – so warm
In the world of dreams
I have my blankets over me;
Galloping across
My vision at night,
A thousand characters.

In Between

Walking to the store
After the rain
Early evening
Winter's light
Is a lighthouse
Peers through the branches of the trees
Almost darkness
Clouds covering a full moon
Then pulling apart
Like curtains on a stage proscenium
A short walk
To sort out sentences
And contemplate flowers
A neighbor and their dog
Transitioning
In between home and corner store
A simple errand
Before the rain.

After the Park Branch Library Poetry Reading

After the Park Branch library poetry reading
The late-night Haight Ashbury
Is still full of music
Poles covered with posters
Forming a tapestry
Fog covers the windows
And it feels like the moors
A tree scraping a third-floor window.
Bird, the poetry magazine's street vendor
Settles on a bench for the night.
I hear the bells
On this side of town;
They are sea bells
Come from the Bay
Ringing into the land.
The Death of the Summer of Love
Was declared many years ago.
Some might interpret the bells as funereal.
I look at the last poems I read
And change two words.
Two lovers are kissing goodnight
On a corner.
The last bus disappears to the station
Waiting to come back again.

Outside My Cottage

  outside my cottage

white Calla lilies   all on a staircase rising

   sound of clothesline pulling in

     the neighbors' laughter

the corridors I live in

    flying orange blankets

on a before-the-rain

     laundry

– coming back to San Francisco –

   i have gone away

     come back,

   gone away

and come back,

pulling across the rope lines.

Albion

Albion Street –
Name for a –
Is it a magical kingdom?
A white cliffed island?
Where Harold Norse
Lived his last days.
Perhaps an island
Surrounded by
Bars, clubs, and
Passing people,
And an old gay poet
Who translated
From Italian
On a little
One block street
Deep in San Francisco's Mission District.
He wanted more,
The real Albion,
Not noise or trash,
A prize he was never given.
But poets still
Recite on the corner
Of Sixteenth Street
And believe in
Whatever
Albion is to them.

The Building on Bartlett Street

I moved to Bartlett Street. Up the building to the third floor. Through the carpeted hallway – half done. My door – the key leading to what's behind it. My one room studio with the picture of the forest in it. I can walk in that forest – reminds me of Mt. Tamalpais and the redwood forests north of San Francisco. Through the glades. Dark and sad sometimes. Like a mood of a man I know. Like walking up the stairs to a dark hallway.

There is a window over my bed. It looks out over a roof third story. At sunset, the sky beams across the window. The colors of radiance, sadness, calmness flash across the window. Purples and pinks and reds – royal hues. I stare at this changing reflection and at the gold in the sky. Beneath this color is a ragged yard, what could be a lawn or a garden, but it is overgrown and wild and locked in by a fence.

The building surrounds me. Its stairs, its little rooms, the noises of parties, screams, fights. I buy my tacos and burritos from Paco's Tacos carrying them back wrapped in aluminum foil. I hear the Spanish spoken, me catching words here and there, understanding these snatches – perhaps, one day, I will understand an entire language.

Barcelona

lady on balcony
stocking in hand
loosely dripping from
her fingers

children going to school
with grandmother
beside them

pigeons on dusty
church steeples

Hydra (1973)

Sailing in between Greek islands
on the ferry,
we arrive
and there is one
room left at
the hotel.
We pretend to be a couple,
and an old woman
takes us down the hall
with a ring of jingling keys.
The morning arrives
with the Blessing of the
Fishing Fleet.
He sleeps
while I walk by
the ceremony,
islanders diving into
the sea
as he dreams
I, walking, walking
find the road around
the island,
walking, walking,
I reach the highest point –
does he dream he
dives into the waves?
I will dive in, too –
The old Greek woman
holds her keys;
when we separate,
holds her black skirts,
shaking her black
skirts, shaking.

Uxmal

I walk through
The Mayan rooms
That the Spanish called
The Nunnery.
I have missed seeing
Some of the serpent carvings
Because of the height of the pyramids' stairs.
The Nunnery's rooms are easier to find,
But the rooms are roped off
Though inside one of the rooms
Lies a live iguana
Who says it is all right
To see an iguana this way.
"My hue is gray today,
I can change my color
To match the walls. We iguanas were here
Before the carvings.
I'm part of nature,
Don't feel bad,
You can see me
As you pass by,"
The iguana lying not so close to the wall
So we can see her without her disappearing.
Or am I anthropomorphizing
About this iguana who has gotten out of the sun
Like the visitors here who scurry to
Huddle beneath the trees
Away from the ceremonial buildings
Scattered into their niches.

Bluebird
September 2020

The bluebird who arrives each year
Perches in my plum tree
And chirps and chirps
As if speaking to me.
I move closer and closer
To the tree
Without the bluebird flying away
Until one last step
When the pretty bluebird
Spreads her wings
And alights on another tree.
Each morning, for a week,
I converse with the bluebird,
Making me think of Maeterlinck
And what is happiness.
One day, the bluebird has flown south.
I know the bluebird will return again next year.

Tamaracks

Traveling by train
Across Canada
End of summer
Early fall
In the northlands
The tamaracks,
Pines that change color
Translating from green to gold.
Native languages
Speak beyond
The train.
Dashes of bright yellow
As the train picks up speed.
The larch of Alberta
And Saskatchewan
Like bright angels
Before the frost arrives
And the gold falls
With the snow.

Call It Bloom

The amaryllis
is three feet tall,
its red blossoms
beginning to open.
At the museum,
Georgia O'Keeffe's
flowers bloom
on canvas.
In the conservatory's gardens,
the tropical plants
wait to be
drawn.

Snow-scape

    Raw
    clarity of
      snow-scape

   iced   and winded

expanses   and steel-
  blue water
    cold air like an animal
    a cold white bear

lumbering from the North
    anything inessential
not there

              blank/clean
    like the floor of a Zen monastery

   one dried stalk sticks up
              above the snow.

Without Warmth

Cold passions
Ice tray cool
A frozen volcano
The memory of fire

Heater on the blink
Frozen faucet
Hot water pipes are running
    The chills.

Thunderstorms in San Francisco

It didn't used to thunder and lightning
In San Francisco,
It was an East Coast
Phenomenon,
And the East Coast
Was my childhood,
Sultry, muggy, hot,
And breaking open,
This city, in my diaspora,
Different from what was normal there
In New York state.

Thunderstorms were to duck.
Thunderstorms here
Seem like larger foghorns
And the lightning strikes
More quickly;
There, in the East, a child
Just needs to run into a house,
Needs to stop her playing;
Here an adult starts
To think about death,
The storm catching
Them on their way
To their work that day.
Weather patterns can change.
These new storms,
Sometimes a beautiful
Drenching,
Makes me pause,
To find home,
A recess,
A shelter.

I pause looking for light,
Trying to run
Into a house
That may no longer
Exist.

My Father's Funeral

In mid-life,
I was like an awkward teenager,
Like many funerals
A rainy day,
In my parents' home, photos of gawky
Long-legged spurts of growth.
I didn't know who the Rabbi was
After years away,
A new Rabbi, a stranger.
Having learned the Jewish traditions
When someone dies,
I threw dirt in the grave,
The inclination to do it quickly
Before the rain came down
Even heavier,
Starting minor landslides
Like the hills in California during winters;
Slipping at the edge in the mud,
There was a gasp.
And someone pulled me back.

Photos

In all the photos
Someone is missing,
The one taking the pictures
On the other side of the camera.
Their perception of me and my sister,
Looking not at all like me,
The photos of me
In what I see as my image
Not what I think.
It's probably my father
Who took most or all of them.
In a file marked family.
Why did we miss taking his photo?
That void in the back
Of negatives
Kept by him
Keeping the family filed
By Father,
Sometimes Mother.
After Father passed
Father moving more into the
Void like moving
Backwards with the
Camera that was
His eye to what
He thought was the
Family in that box
In the closet's cabinet.

The Presses

My grandfather,
Who was the Editor of a newspaper,
Grandpa Harry, took me to the *Forward* paper's building.
There was a large room with the rolling presses turning,
Sheets of paper churning
Caught up in a huge design,
Could walk through this
Field of ink and words.
I knew there was more to this,
The writers' offices
But this I remember most,
The machinery lifting up the papers,
And creating their existence,
The wonder of having one's own press,
My own little journal
Going to a printer
And picked up in a car;
One poetry editor
Told me his dream was
To study printing
And have a press of his own.

Cherry Soup

If I picked enough cherries,
my mother would make cherry soup,
cause in Europe
people made fruit soups,
cold, sweet or sour.
I needed enough cherries to fill a pot,
needed to climb up a ladder
to the cherry tree branches,
find one flat spot on
a small rise,
so the pot and I didn't tumble.
No one I ever knew ate cherry soup,
experimenting in the kitchen
like with red melodies of peasant
women in Hungarian
country village
kitchen home.
Green and white checkered tablecloth,
open sky,
small steps on raked ladder,
enough cherries,
a little more cherries,
stir, if I picked enough cherries,
Mother made cherry soup.

David

Mi esposo
thinks of the woody wagon
he had years ago
as we climb up mountains
in Colorado;
he thinks of
giving away free food
from the back of the wagon
in a Boulder park.
Mi esposo
played baseball
with the
kids on the
Chicago Southside
back when Minnie Miñoso
played outfield.
Walking through the spring grass now
we find a pickup game in the same park,
find young ones
to give away a glove.
Mi esposo
voted for the
fourth party,
or maybe
the fifth,
Mi esposo
drives his
twenty year
old station
wagon in Oakland,
and San Francisco
where artists in their twenties
try to live

and burn
succumbing to smoke and fire.
Mi esposo and I
drive to Ludlow
and watch a train
by the same tracks
where fires burned
on miners'
shacks,
we see
the statue of the mother
holding her children,
who died in the Ludlow massacre,
watch the tumbleweed
turn over and over,
asking why
in what could be desolate
and sad is
so strangely beautiful.

Strabismus

Once a week,
I watch the wheel spin around,
And try to see pictures
Come together
As one,
But they stay
Apart because one eye
Is on its own path.
My sister called me pirate
When I was three
But I don't remember that.
At seven, I hid the eye patch
Behind trees;
Later in life
I went to therapy
Where if you
Can figure out the letters
On the chart
By guessing
What you can see
Then you are seeing
But she thought
Jazz confused one,
Perhaps she was right
And I like being confused,
I still remember the wheel
Spinning round and around
Then my eye decided to wander.
It hadn't wandered to the side before,
I decided to keep it that way,
After all, it was real,
It did what it wanted to,
A friend

Said symmetry is overrated
But others said they didn't know where I was looking
And worst of all, it was weird.
And then I was told about a doctor,
A surgeon who mostly operated on children,
Children who might be called weird
But this was scary, being an adult,
Mickey Mouse in the office
Didn't help,
And then I woke up
And my eye was back in the center
And when did I see
That my surgeon
Had cerebral palsy or polio
When he was young?

Lurilla and Lavender Girl

Everyone knew Lurilla,
Lurilla went to city meetings
In her purple feathered hat,
She smiled and said hello
83 years old
So small in a walker
When death hit her in the street
Just like that.
And there's this street girl
No one really knew
With the lavender hair
Trying to be like Pearl
But their colors kind of matched
And so did the sky
The sun turning pink
When the fires came by,
Lurilla at eighty-three
Run over
Except for her
Purple feathered hat
That rolled and rolled.
Never knew the street girl's name
Her lavender hair still under
A lamp pole,
Lurilla and Lavender Girl
Both came from the South,
Could tell from the tone,
At a young age,
That I did know.
Between Lurilla and Lavender Girl
Their paths crossed once…
They each exchanged a word,
"I like your purple feathered hat,"
"I like your hair of lavender, Girl."

Corky

Where did Corky go?
Real name Elisa
In your black jeans
And heavy black boots
Favorite song "Queen Jane Approximately"
By Bob Dylan.
I was 16 in 1965
And never heard Dylan before.
Were you Queen Jane
Refusing to wear a dress
On a camp girls' trip?
I've looked for you
But never found you.
Did you disappear
From Long Island
To gay bars
On dark New York streets
Or another city
Like London, San Francisco?
In the old days,
Did you not want to come out,
Or did you contemplate suicide
Or do it?
Were you what
Some called a dyke?
If you ride a bike,
I could see you
On the Dyke March
With your leather boots.
Queen Jane Approximately,
Are you Queen Jane?
Or are you happier as a trans
Finally happier?
Approximately Queen Jane

You

Who is the You
In all the poems I read?
The You who is your love
The one you wait for
Are you the you
And another you
Is reaching to you
Beyond the page?
Do all the yous
Meet in a metaphor?
I can visualize
Them all.
There are the beautiful yous,
The yous like the furies,
The evil you
Creating injustice,
Now chastised forever
On the page
Or a mother
A father
Who lives in the afterlife.
What are their names?
All the nameless yous in poems,
Someone's child,
A lost friend,
Gone before their time,
Spirits to be addressed to,
I am someone else's you,
You are someone else's you.

Escaping Fire

We try and escape
what is real,
run from fires
that singe
what one believes,
are caught
in lies,
and untruths,
forests burn,
the sun
turns red,
smoke covers
and clouds vision,
a bird listens
to another bird,
and flies
over the trees
to seek breath.

Under

If I had a white horse
I would name her Pearl,
And ride on sands
And in wedding processions,
And invite all the poets
In San Francisco
To parade with me and Pearl
In my dream
In a hospital room
Where everyone wears white.
So, I have become mistaken,
Thinking the white horse
Named Pearl
Has come to my bedside
But when sleep
Makes me go deeper,
A black horse
Named Black Pearl
Goes down to
The River Styx,
Throws back his head
And neighs
And whispers
There is only one way
Out of here
And that is on my back
So hold on
And we each will live
Another day.

Skeleton

On the edge of the Mission,
In front of St. Luke's hospital,
Windy day by the bus stop,
A black garbage bag
Is blown across the road,
A skeleton on one side
Of the frayed bag.
The faded bones dance
Lifted high
Flying up to a low cloud
And swooping down
Underneath a blue truck.
My bus pulls in
And carries me away,
Death flickering
Through the windows' long array,
Like a flip book kineograph
Death dancing on the hood
In the hood
As I travel on.

Woman Having a Mask Made of Her Face

Why am I here?
She fits the plaster mask over my face,
Leaving two straws in my nose
To breathe,
I am tenuously connected
To living
Through my breath,
They call these death masks.
It will continue when I'm gone.
But this was for a drama class.
To use for a mask?
To represent your subconscious?
The other you?
But now, I wait inside
The person inside the mask,
As though there are
Two of us.
I am careful
Not to disturb
My mask.
The mask is white plaster.
An undercoat keeps the mask
From staying on my face.
How is each layer of
What could be skin different?
My face cut off from
The outside world
My ears strain to hear.
The room is silent.
My mouth does not move
In the mask.
The mold removed,
I see the light again.

Many years later,
The white plaster crumbles
On the shelf
Where it lain for years.

Playing Solitaire

Sometimes one lives as though in
Solitary confinement,
One's own partner
In solitaire,
Living within one's heart.
Leaving fantasies
Alone, if one can ever
Be completely alone
As faces float through
The mind,
And dreams crowd in
At night.
I deal to myself,
And the cards come back
To me,
Padding the silence,
With my mirror,
Myself.

My Woman's Id

Maybe I am free
Now to dance on
Cobblestones,
Dance floors,
Threshing places,
To sacrifice
Wheat to Greek gods,
Being a woman.

Untitled

Little girl
Going to be a woman
Dancing and spinning
In the space that is
Still yours.

Sunrise Ritual

Twist, wind, and braid,
Fold the hair
High off the neck,
Tuck it under
Ribbon smooth,
Teach it
To obey
Patterns.
Knead it and weave it
Breadbasket comfortable;
Coil it into a pot.
Let it carry water
From every fountain
In every market place
Where women stop to gather,
Stop to talk,
Stop to let their hair down –
Down over their ears, over their shoulders,
Over their breasts, over their bellies,
Over the earth, growing,
Growing into one long strand.

To Be a Witch

How I would like to be a witch
If witches could do what
People say they do.
To fly over
Housetops
Over the Victorians
With bay windows.
Were witches
Really midwives
Helping as needed,
Women who came in
The night and tended
With potions and spells,
Words that cured,
Organic herbs
That I can find
On the edge of fields and meadows?
The healer witch.
The magician witch, why in black
With a pointed hat
On a broom
And a cat, also black,
Just a caricature.
Yet I know she flew.
Let me ride on her broom,
Drink her brew,
Sing in a circle,
Become a witch, a wicca,
Rise out of the flames
That burned me,
On trial,
Take off the chains
That imprisoned me,
Inhale the smoke of her healing potions.

The Woman Climber on Annapurna

High cliffs
View sweeping
Into cold territories.
She climbed
Into dangerous
Crevices,
Her ropes and knots
Entwined;
Some souls stay up there,
The mountain's extensions
Jutting into the sky,
Nepalese prayer flags
Brightly flapping,
The wind tumbles down
Her thousands of steps.

Wild Nights

I said to Melen
That being born in March
She was being born in the season of flowers,
Miniature daisies and white plum blossoms,
But during some Marchs
The storms rammed in too
Blowing trees down
Letting garbage cans
Roll riotously through the street
And roughing up the soft edges
Of pastel views.
During a march of storms
Wide-eyed babies
Flow out on high tides;
They see the world from bridges
As angels beat their wings,
And we party
Celebrating
Birth
On wild nights and days.

Crossing the River

My grandmother said
I dreamed that I crossed a
river without a bridge.
I was only seven,
the low mountains behind me.
I was told
the river takes one to
America.
I remembered
I wore a sheepskin
jacket with embroidered
flowers
to wear on cold nights.
Did I want to leave?
There were eight of us.
We left a few at a time
from a village with
paprika plants
and one street.
What would we
pack into a suitcase?
My sister Pauline
took her cuckoo clock,
Henry his books,
Louisa two violins,
Laura, a remembered recipe for pogacsa,
her butter cookies.
I, Ida, was the smallest one
with my crochet needles.
The ocean was large.
It was so many years ago,
yet what I dream of
is how I crossed a
river without a
bridge.

Stations

If we could take trains
Backwards to where we
Were born,
To where we came from,
Pulling into a welcoming
Depot;
Find the right station
For the day or night.
Maybe, the ornate gilded one,
The only palace we can all partake of,
Or the tiny cabin
With friendly people in the cold
On the way to hills,
Or a flow of commuters,
At the suburban ticket booth
Looking to go to bigger cities,
That slice of terminal,
Embryonic,
Returns you to a bubble
Back in time,
For anyone who has left
Their station,
For stations
That are still left.

Wall of Roses

I have a wall of roses.
One does not think of roses as a wall.
Walls have moats and turrets.
My wall of roses is a bower alongside a garden.
And sometimes a welcomed visitor will come,
Will want to come in,
To climb over,
To be let in,
To appear from next door,
To fall into a yard, forgetting about private property,
Lines of ownership,
Parts of the bower falling in the rain,
Leaves coming down, cats wandered in,
Birds landing.
So, it isn't odd when an unexpected visitor appears.
They say walls are used in war to keep people out.
But this bower of roses is a different kind of wall.

The Peace Rose

I was named for Peace,
and planted
in a glass house
where nations are told not to
throw stones,
in a rock garden
in a desert
where I am the
only flower,
where my soft
light color
disappears among
the bright red,
I apologize for thorns
that continue to
prick
next to petals
that fall and
fade,
I am such a
vain rose
too pretty
to dance with
you
but sometimes
I do.

War or Peace?

I slope down into the beach
On an angled walk
Something in my head
Keeps ticking
Like an aneurism that may open soon;
This uncomfortable type of death
Is a strange whisper
Different than the
Rampages
Of hyenas and wasps,
There's so many kinds of history
All the legions that
Devastated cities
And the piercing desperation
In a child's eyes
Looking out from a wall.
There's my lonely walk to a library
With people lying on the steps
And trying to look above it all
Seeing a kaleidoscope
Of the world's people
And there
Is a small stage with mimes near the church of St. Francis.
There are steps from the bottom
Of the city to the top,
To the stars
If only we knew how to climb.
The enemy of the heart can cling
Like a lover feeding poison.
I'm looking for a musical progression
Where the interaction of harmonies do not clash.

The Five of Us

A little mouse lives
Behind a piano
Perhaps for years
Avoiding confrontations
With the cat,
A spider
Lingers over
An old computer
On a windowsill,
The dog only observing
Meanders
Through the
House,
Old enemies
Live unspoken
Truces
In this no man's
Land
38th Parallel
War zone
Of conscientious
Peace.

Firmament

A backward F in a Viking alphabet
Is A
Though it looks like
A sixteenth note
How it is pronounced
I don't know,
As I try to hear their words.
There was a group making decisions,
A council,
In a circle of
Runestones in the
Forest by a lake
Miles away from a modern Swedish city
The beauty of the forest
And engravings of the stones
If warriors and sailors
Here there seems to be peace and spirituality
At least in this moment
Above me is the firmament.

In the Forest

In the forest,
Three little bears
On a mountain
Looking down towards the fire,
Flames crossing a river,
Coyote runs to a city
Mountain lion, tail on fire,
Swims in the river,
Bears' paws on earth
Getting hot,
Fire retardant rains down,
Then rain comes
Three weeks and the fire stops.
A bird finds one charred tree to land on,
Three little bears
Are crying, the forest is crying,
Birds leave messages from the whole earth,
Flowers in Greece,
Kangaroos in Australia.
Is it too late
As the animals come out of hiding?
Answers in the wind
And sun,
The coyote raises her head,
Lifting her voice.

Glen Park

The coyote in Glen Park
Has been tricking the rest of us;
She lives in the city
Yet in a canyon
That rises above
An underground stream
That fools the concrete.
The coyote like
An invisible apparition,
We receive warnings
And we do not see her
But at dawn or twilight
Might catch her shadow.
She cares for her pups
Hidden in a den;
She has found a home
Where many are homeless.
She may howl at the moon
On foggy nights
Calling it out
Behind the leaves.
Her tracks are parallel
To mine
Can I hear her steps?
She climbs the red and purple
Nasturtium covered
Canyon's walls;
She sees us
We do not see her.
We've been waiting for each other
As elusive as an oxymoron,
In the city canyon.

Ten Lakes

There are ten lakes in San Francisco's Golden Gate Park
And Lake Merced,
Mountain Lake,
I keep walking through
The backwoods of Golden Gate Park,
I want to see each of the ten lakes
Hidden away from the ocean.
When Covid gets better
I'll keep walking
And when Covid stops,
I'll keep taking walks.
Because now I know
This city better,
It's not the city of sidewalks,
It's the woods and water,
The bird I call the white duck
In Stern Grove's pond.
Paths that have above ground roots
That rise like hills,
Aromas of eucalyptus, bay laurel, and pine.
Round brown acorns
When pounded, natives made flour,
A willow canopy.
Further and further into this forested world,
So far that coyotes have made their home here,
A collage of leaves.
And even along Oyster Bay,
Where each month,
An industrial park arises,
One colossal building at a time
Finally surrounding all of the Bay
Except a path along the water,
Where a faded educational sign

Depicts an avocet,
And there it is, yes,
I can see the
Tall orange bird
Flying over the bay,
So, I keep walking.

Earth Day

They gathered to celebrate
    The earth
   The snow-tipped
Feathers of swans
Brushing like haiga
   Strokes.

The White Ducks

They were always there
Two large white ducks
Together.
A couple it appeared,
Loyal to one another,
Floating in the Stern Grove pond
Near the other
Brown and yellow ducks
But paddling in their own aura
Of togetherness;
If they were apart on one day
I looked for the other one,
It always eventually joined
With its partner,
Swans I knew
Mated for life,
And though these two
Were not long necked swans
They were almost so,
Making me think of my mate
And recall my wedding at City Hall
For the fifteen-dollar certificate
Where we and others could gather under
The grand dome
And marble staircase officiated
By a kind mustachioed man,
But back to the ducks.
For one day,
Across the pond,
One duck was
No longer there,
And the next week,
No longer with

Its partner.
It would not fly away.
Had it grown old and died?
Or had it been killed?
The other duck swims near the
Rest of the ducks now,
A little apart, but near.
Is he or she sad?
Now, the white duck
Doesn't seem quite as elegant – just
One of the other ducks.
Maybe my fate
One day to join
A pack for comfort
And keep on swimming.

The Vole

The vole waddles along
The bottom of the fence
In Stern Grove.
The vole is smaller than a mole
And creeps slowly
Not rambling
He makes his walk
Deliberate
Turtlelike
Unafraid
My fifteen-year-old dog
Today is oblivious
To the vole's journey
But what about my journeys
That have gone much farther
Than the straight line
Forward moving vole,
His goal ambitiously ahead,
His target to enter the woods
Blocked by the fence
To his ultimate
Destination
Yet unaware of the
Park's distractions
The vole keeps moving
Onward.
My journeys took me
On travels
Took my mind on imaginary journeys
Reading Joyce and Tolstoy
And flights of fancy
Instead of a linear
Life that went

From one benchmark
To the next
Unlike the little round vole
That clings tenaciously
To his mission
Until he reaches
The hole in the fence
Where it opens
Into the woods.
And now the vole
Disappears,
Returning safe into his
Underground burrow
And like lightning
That strikes once
The vole is gone
Like a stone dropping
Deep in a well,
The vole is gone,
Missing him like a friend
Away from my
Peering curious eyes.

Going to Jupiter

(Jupiter, Florida)

Going to see manatees,
Manatees swim in the hot water
Of the local power plant,
Their mural
Praising the manatees' choice,
In bright colors,
And comic style
Next to the African-American
Community
That is placed living next
To the power plant.
Wondering when we drive away
How any of us
Are going to survive
On this strange planet?

We Seahorses

The two of us
Dance with
Our manes
Close together
Turning bright gold.
We entice,
Happily we mate,
Soon after, I
Bring all those eggs
To place in his pouch,
And off I go,
Me, the female one
To live my life
As the guy in my life
Takes care of all the growing little seahorses;
I do visit daily
What the biologists call
"Morning greetings,"
Swish my tail a bit
Shake my mane,
And then take a swim.
So nice of him
And evolution.

Diatoms

Under a microscope
Diatoms appear
Kaleidoscopic
Like snowflakes
Floating in sea water
Beautiful algae
In the ocean
That you don't see
Creating half of the world's oxygen:
Breathe.

After Coming Back from Big Sur

The trees are breathing
soft night-time
noises,
each black vibration
rafting
back and forth
over rain-dreams
up river
down sky;
racoon star-steps
creep pleasant
on the toes
of pine;
and, three deer,
shy as I,
peer past
wood's table
to the day
behind.

The Tall Trees

When I walk
Through the park
And see the tall trees
In their twisted shapes
Reaching and diving
From the windy days
I think of the trees
In "The Wizard of Oz,"
How these trees could turn
Into living voices, too;
They came alive
And walked and talked,
Trees more companions
Than people these days
For more than a year,
The redwood and eucalyptus,
Their height
Overwhelming.

Strategy

So much has been
Cleared away,
Thrown away, old papers,
Old life, lives, rotting food.
Boxes full of toy monkeys
And birds.
Remembrances of poets
Who lived in trees
And sang with angels
On holidays of their choosing.
Sometimes I wish for it all back.
Other times, it disappears
Like a Chekhovian chord
Fading in a forest.
Even when I make a plan,
The plan outsmarts me.
Or a pile, like a nightmare,
Becomes tamed,
A little pony that can be ridden.
I search for a strategy.
A camel, with water for
A long trip with stops at
The next oasis.

Romance of the Porch

There is a room that
Can't be named right.
It was the old porch,
It says it is a room
But it wants old encounters
And a window that looks out
To a long tunnel,
Sees flowers
Tries tuning
To get the right note
On each peg,
It has a new window
That magnifies the view,
It sees streets
Where there are only cafes
And music,
A boat ride,
Along a river
A meeting under a bridge,
A suspension bridge in Algiers
Laced with gardenias.
There is a room
That I can't name right.
It is the old porch,
The study, the back room;
It studies all the back porches
In the neighborhood,
Its stairs
Descend into a land of shadows.

The Feral Puppy

Each month at the full moon my puppy of two years feels the effects of the moon on him, begins to act strange, as he must go out and dance, and sing high pitches, and during the winter storms, he sleeps pressed against a rattling pane of glass and is wild for two days tugging at my arm. When it rains he rolls over and sleeps curled warm puppy intuition. He was born deep in the Tenderloin and is street smart, flashing golden bravado, but frightened, whimpers like a puppy, and can be entranced by the pull of the tides, by a bright full moon.

Why I Can't Spell Graffiti and Other Musings

The fs and ts alternate
In my mind
The ts temperamental
Fs fickle
Artistically illegal
Claiming hidden spaces
Boarded up buildings,
Tags not quite words
Italian highwire
Perhaps the chosen artform
Of skateboarding teenagers,
Now out of school,
Honing their skills
While marauding down hills,
Swishing across corners,
With their best buddies,
Who meet every afternoon
In an empty schoolyard
Leaping over a closed fence,
Elegantly flying and hopping like birds
While I write poetry,
Known as creative writing
Where grammar and spelling is optional.

Communication

The ant crosses
The manuscript pages
That I am typing.
The black letters are about
The same size
As the ant from
Head to toe,
Their feet canter across
The white pages
Onto the desk and back again,
Then disappearing;
Does my ant
Take in any of the
Poetry beneath its feet?
He or she revolves
From place to place
On the desk's edge
To beyond the modem and wires,
Today making trails
With its own
Encoded language.

Learning the Alphabet

We drive to sing in
A choral concert;
The children sit in
The back seat.

"A, B, C, D, E, F, G,"
Liza, three years old,
Begins the letters,
They run into each other
Going fast,
Then not entirely
Definite.

Her brother, Owen, four,
Wants them faster,
– Faster, faster, –
They race to
See who knows
Their letters better and quicker.

When did I learn the alphabet?
That time of letters
Preceding writing
Forms
In front of me.
And
We arrive
At the hall
Our destination
Where the adults
Will sing their words.

Lesson in Jazz

Inside the apartment
I had my singing lesson
in jazz,
and outside on
the street were the
noises of
working on the
road,
the clattering
shattering
beat of the machines.
Improvising
inside the room,
I soloing over
the tap circling,
drumming on
my ear drums,
rapping with music
on that street
inside and out.

Bajone's

So many years ago,
We went to hear jazz,
Bajone's was painted
Black at first,
Then painted red,
And the Meat Market Coffee House
Changed from brown to pink,
Small businesses
That allowed homeless people
Around the edges,
They not being that different,
And jazz musicians, poets, and street people,
Merging together,
Bob Kaufman wandering into Bajone's
To whisper poems
Both black and red,
And labor too,
The Poets' Union
Met at Bajone's,
It didn't last long,
Was it chaos?
Or was that jazz?

Miles

My brother gave me my first
Miles Davis records,
his old Miles Davis records,
hard to believe
that one could no longer
have use for such a collection.
I certainly knew what to do
    with them –
Kind of Blue for dreaming,
for sad and slow,
Sketches of Spain for traveling,
for passion, for a culture
of romance.
I'd heard other jazz –
but it wasn't modern;
my seventeen-year-old
life was now capable
of going to museums of
modern art, going to
international movies, listening to
Miles Davis, wearing
my brother's too large
shirts even if the Beat
era was over.
My brother got married and stopped
going on dates to jazz clubs –
but I was cool;
with Miles I could go out on a limb.

Love Sessions

Trying to connect,
Feel like want to meet someone,
Jazz was boiling
Like hot water,
I could throw myself into it
And sizzle,
The place on the corner
With tables that elbows
Leaned across
Erasing the boundaries
Filling in the spaces
I always went there at dusk
And it felt like being in a parade,
Felt soft like felt
Rambled into it,
Jumbled together,
People and music
Stewing like soup.

In Transit

So long ago, one summer in Chicago,
We both had studied anthropology,
He was a taxi driver
And I was going back to school
And we explored
Transit stations
As anthropologists
Noting each mini-culture
As the trains
Rose up as El trains
In a windy city
But I observed him, too,
Making notes of
Incongruities to
My idea of perfection,
I as cold as Lake Michigan's winter ice,
Throwing that love away
Like the blowing paper
That the news racks had
That the leaving trains
Stirred,
Passengers waiting for a train to come,
And we explored each other
Feeling the heat like from a passing train
The tracks not running parallel;
It's not regret or being sorry, but
Like tracks that were broken.
Now, standing beside the trolley tracks
Thinking about parallel lives
In front of San Francisco's old wooden houses
Wondering about the past,
And tracks that won't intersect.

The Trieste Café

Solitary sitters
Each at small round tables
With mosaics
The Trieste is the same
When one walks in
After years
Even recognized
By the same counterman.
Some of the tables'
Dwellers turn and
Speak with one
Another.
Even sitting apart it is as
Though the Trieste is
An orchestra
With each of the instruments, like the
Many colored tiles on the tables.
The menu is
The same,
The prices are not
But customers
Scribble away in
Their notebooks,
Or huddle over
Their books,
Even those at
Computers appear
Literary. On the jukebox
A tenor from
An opera being
Played holds a
Long note.

In the Workers' Café

In Florence,
Lunchtime,
In the workers' café,
Seeing into the workings of
The open kitchen,
The steaming and fryings,
The bubbling pots and pans,
Behind the food market,
Several avenues away
From the nearest Michelangelo statue,
And the Medici tomb,
Workers in blue coveralls
Like tools in a tool belt,
The Commedia clatters
With forks and spoons,
And talk, and eating, and talk,
Then, the workers' vanguard
Goes back
To the factory
And the rest rise and flow,
As a bell chimes
For the afternoon shift
To start.

Marble, Colorado

Above the river,
is the old marble quarry.
Colorado-born children hike easily
as I edge along with ropes
on the blade-thin path looping
high over the river.
Slabs of marble are caught in the rapids,
some as large as rams
on rocks like animals in traps.
Opulence is overshadowed
by the hills and tall pines and clear sky.
Once the quarry was busy with workers,
now it is as silent
as a hushed rabbit in a bush.
The river flow is barely slowed
by the heaps that sit
and are grand, beautiful, and
broken.

The Lights on Broadway

Broadway in Oakland
Is a muted shade
At 7 PM winter
Evening, a day
After winter solstice
When we think the lights are brighter,
It is still cold.
I turn onto Seventeenth Street.
The Thai and Vietnamese restaurants are open
With plates of food,
And the homeless man prepares to settle
In the union building's doorway
As large as a small courtyard,
A luxurious outdoor apartment.
I wait for the key to arrive.
If I don't have a specific key
The seven union members amassing
Will have to camp out on the hallway floor.
The man knows more about the doors than I do
As he explains the locks and keys and rules
Of the building's landlord owners.
Acting as a guide to the inner sanctum
Away from the now rainy evening
And the lights on Broadway.

Buried Treasure

    For Cliff McIntire the founding editor of
    the *Haight Ashbury Literary Journal*

So, there is this fish
Given to me as a gift,
And then,
There was a file cabinet
Behind a desk
Stuffed with papers,
And now, a fish
Stuffed with peppers,
Finally, time to move
All the drawers
With photos and poems,
Poems pouring into my arms,
And a little orange notebook,
It's my friend Cliff's
Written with a fountain pen,
Pale blue ink,
Some of the poems blurred with water.
On the first pages,
Cliff explains his cookbook,
Because after
Prison, mental hospitals,
The Korean War,
He started a novel
But the novel wasn't coming
So there is this fish, and
Instead of a novel,
Cliff's recipe for
Pescado Vera Cruz;
I don't like fish,
But I was given one,
And in my drawer

Under drawings and books,
Is that buried treasure,
The little orange cookbook
Forty years after
Cliff died, found collapsed on
A Haight Ashbury sidewalk,
And this fish was good,
Cliff McIntire,
An adopted name;
I think he was
Sicilian,
and this fish I liked.

Louis'

The gaggle of old friends
Goes to Louis' every Sunday
Louis' hangs over the rocks
Along the Pacific Ocean
The seals socialize on the rocks
The sunsets each night at Louis'.
If you go to Louis'
No need to think of
Million-dollar houses,
The old friends have homes
With flaking paint from
The sea wind,
They are on the sleepy beach
Where the nineteenth century
Came and went,
Battered sculptures
And public swimming pools
And 1950s neon playgrounds
But the group lived
All through it
As they lived through one
Or two wars, and now whatever is next,
3 men and 2 women
A small dog with a
White face,
Down the road
The old boarded up veterans' bar
Is repaired as a bistro,
Its Depression era WPA
Mural touched up.
Louis' incongruously
Serves Manhattan clam chowder
In San Francisco,

Tiny box facing the
Ocean rocks,
One day islands
Unseen in the fog
The next day revealed,
Louis' perches precariously
On the edge of the continent.

Mesmerized

I didn't think Mt. Olympus was real
A creation for the gods to dwell on
Yet I was invited to go there,
North from Athens
On the local bus,
Through a rainstorm
Olive tree after olive tree
Let off the bus
At the station change
We arrived at one tiny bus stop
With a monk in a habit
Smoking a cigar,
Nothing to be seen
Until the rain cleared
And the entire range of mountains appeared
From out of the clouds
Each moment more magnificent
The craggy fingers of
Gorges descending,
Peak after peak revealed
Of the Olympus Range
Pointing towards the heavens,
Just the two of us and one monk
On his way to the town of Litochoro's
Monastery,
The town square nearly empty
That afternoon
For storm warnings,
The bus pulling closer and closer to the mountains;
We watched,
Mesmerized.

Ocean

So much carried on my back,
Ships with produce,
Ships with human cargo,
The wrinkles of tides
Of my face,
Clashing together,
In deep storms,
Linking continents.
I've heard
Sadness,
Witnessed torture,
Seen those fleeing
From one continent
To the next,
Tides and time
Lapping at shores,
Whales used for oil,
And otters at play
In red tides.
I am the ocean
This planet Earth
Filled with water
And ice that
Is melting
Home to the earliest
Living creatures,
Creatures of the sea
Who live in my belly
Who crave
Nourishment
And give it,
Floating
Like angels

Under what
A person can
See
And only
Dream of.

Acknowledgements:

"Paul Robeson's Voice" *Blue Collar Review*

"David" *Blue Collar Review*

"Cold" in the anthology *Fog and Light*

"Synchronicity" Friends of the San Francisco Public Library Poem of the Day

"The Peace Rose" *Haight Ashbury Literary Journal*

"Call it Bloom" *Poetry Pacific*

"To Ronnie Goodman" *Street Sheet*

"Wild Nights" *Poetry Pacific*

"Glen Park" *The Avocet*

"Ten Lakes" *The Avocet*

"In the Forest" *The Avocet*

"The White Ducks" *The Avocet*

"The Vole" *The Avocet*

"Snow-scape" *The Avocet*

"Tamaracks" *The Avocet*

"Miles" *North Coast Literary Review*

About the Author

Alice Elizabeth Rogoff grew up in New Rochelle, New York. She has lived in San Francisco since 1971. She has a BA in Anthropology from Grinnell College, MAs in English: Concentration Creative Writing, and Drama from San Francisco State University and a Certificate in Labor Studies from City College, San Francisco. Her poetry book *Mural* won a Blue Light Book Award. From the San Francisco Arts Commission, she received a commission for a poetry project. She has been an Editor of the *Haight Ashbury Literary Journal* since 1984. Her poems and stories have been published in many literary magazines and anthologies including the *Garland Court Review*, *Pudding Magazine*, *So to Speak*, *Caveat Lector*, the *Noe Valley Voice*, *Pandemic Puzzle Poems*, *Fog and Light – San Francisco Through the Eyes of the Poets Who Live Here*, *Giving Voice* (LaborFest Writers), and songs in *Alte* by *Jewish Currents*. She volunteers for the San Francisco Living Wage Coalition. She is a member of PEN America, San Francisco Senior and Disability Action, and Save the Manatee Club.

www.ingramcontent.com/pod-product-compliance
Lightning Source LLC
Chambersburg PA
CBHW031157160426
43193CB00008B/401